The R[illegible]

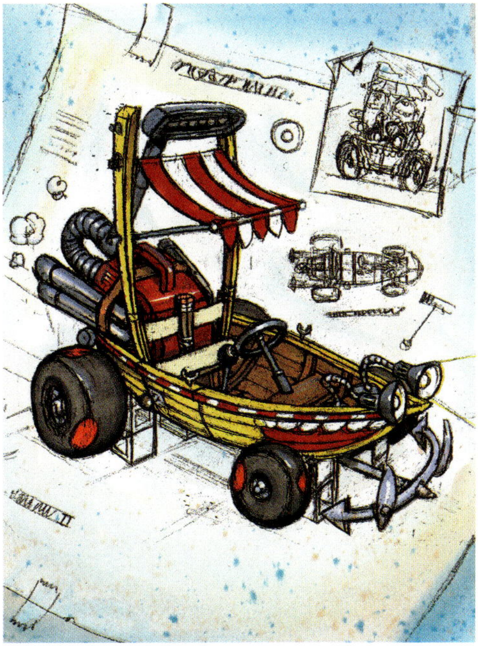

Illustrated by Andrew Trimmer

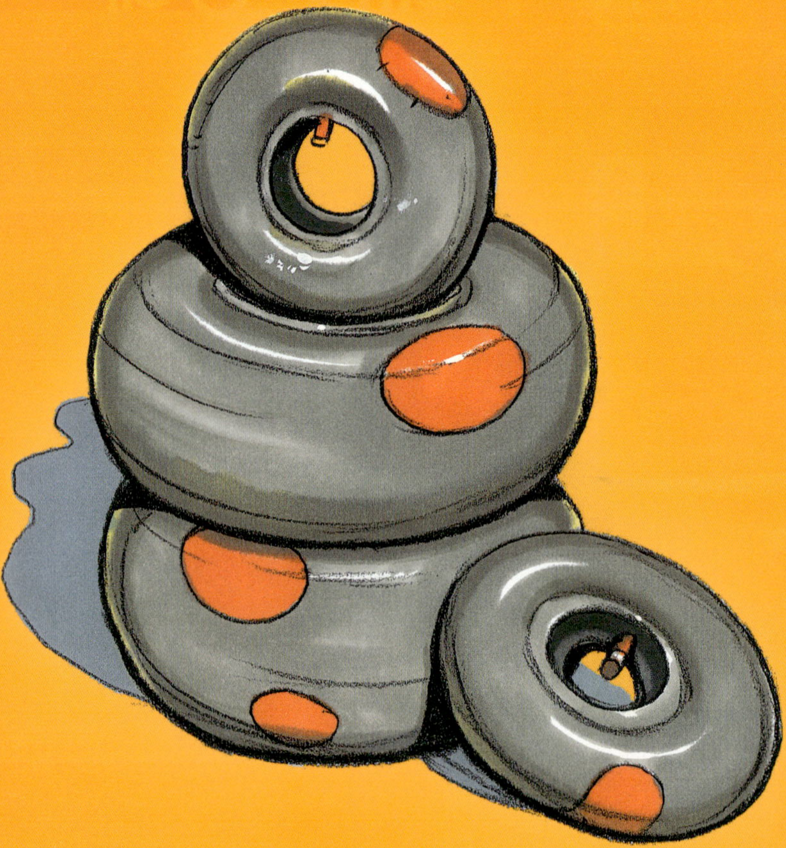

We put on
the wheels.

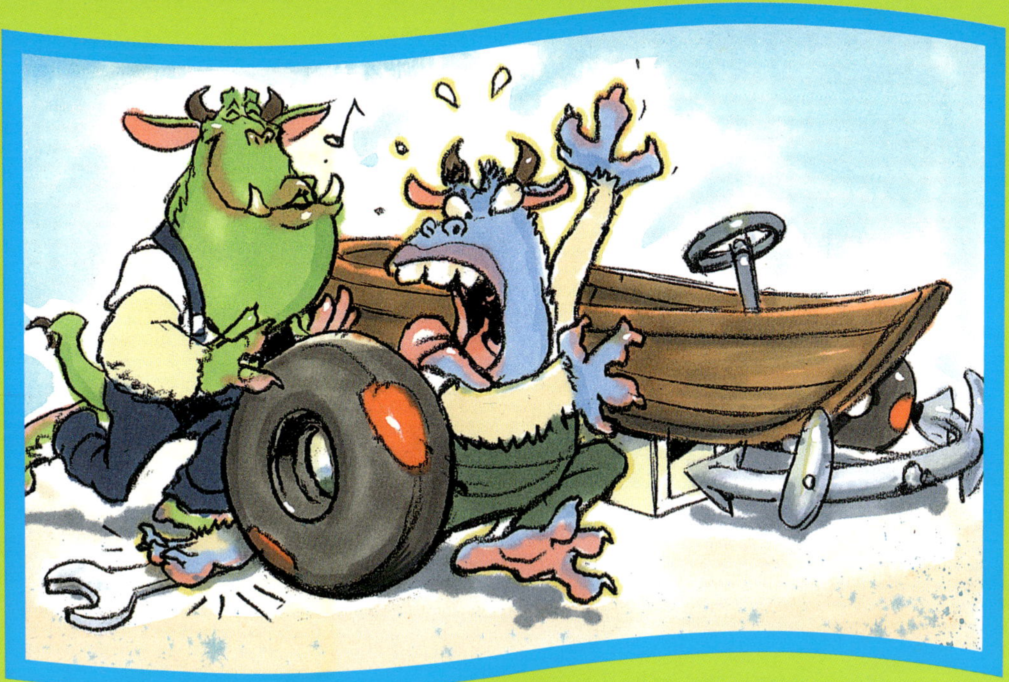

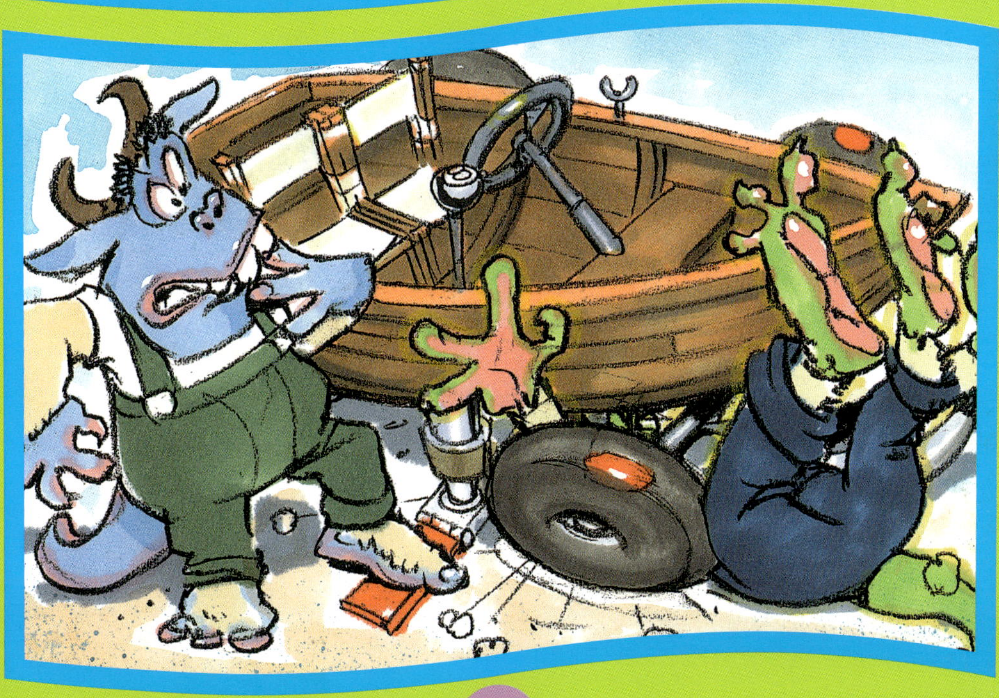

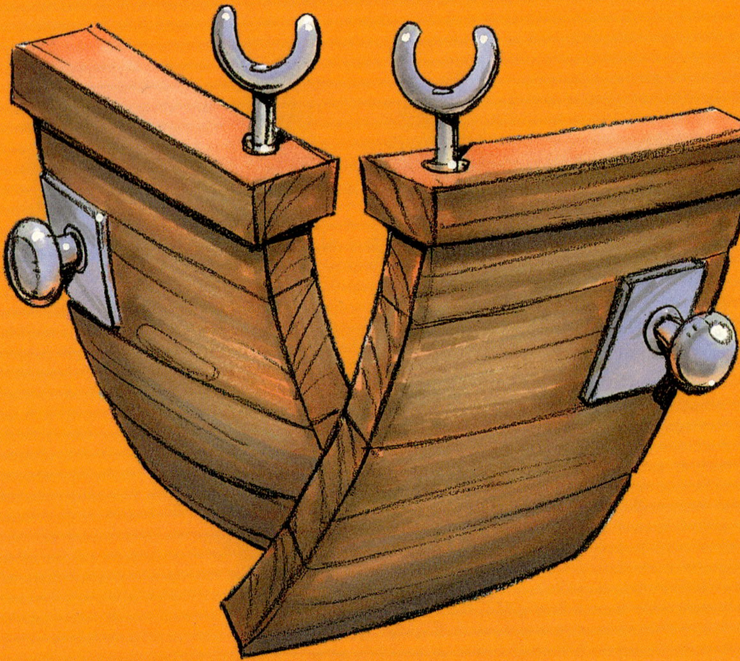

We put on
the doors.

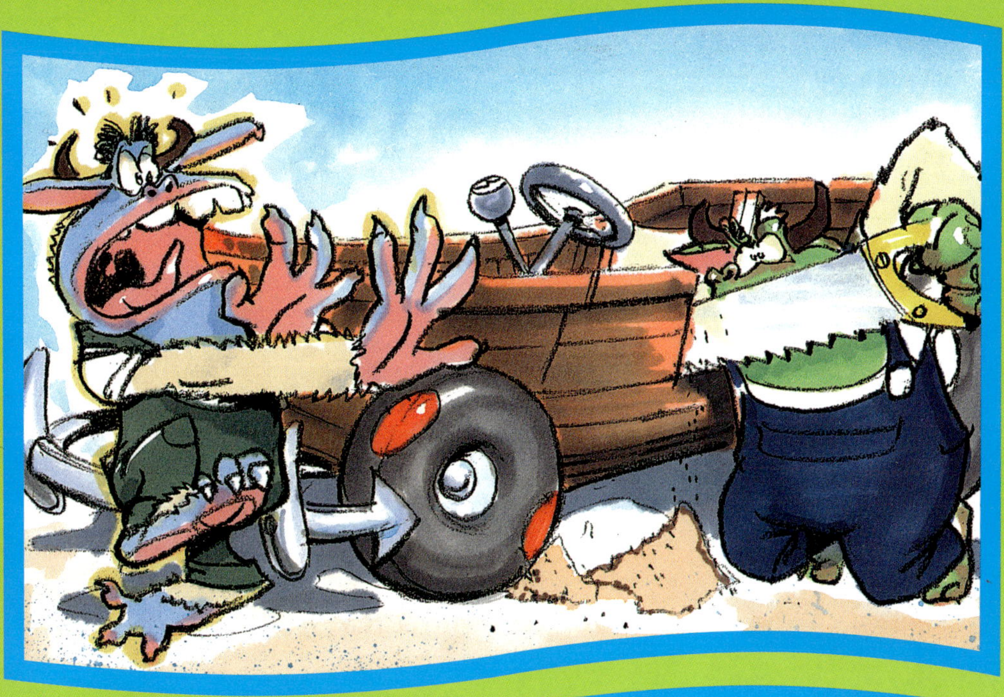

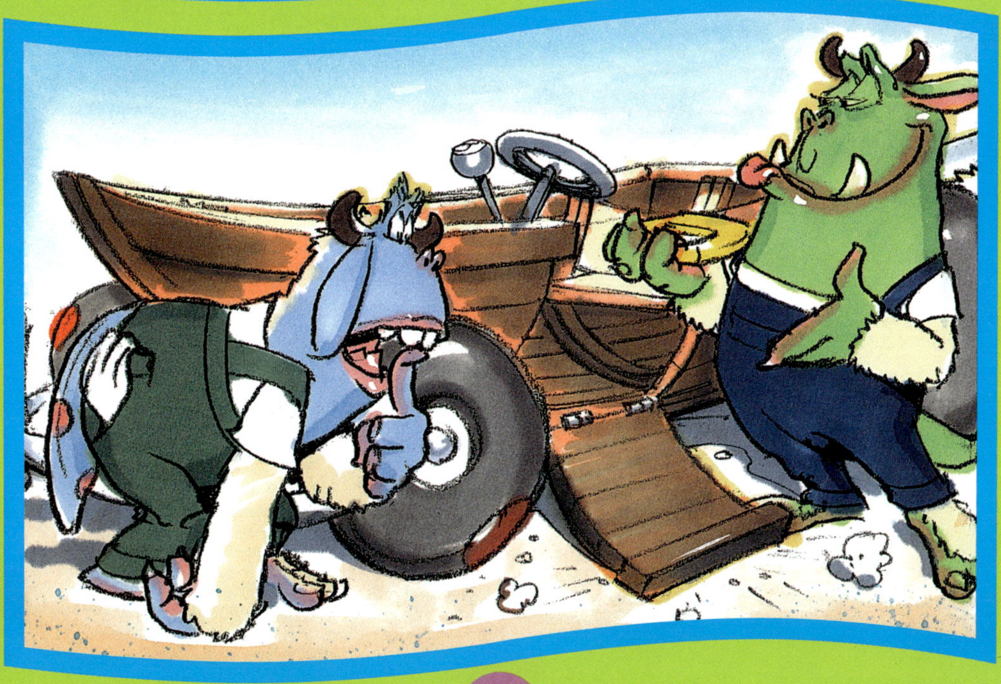

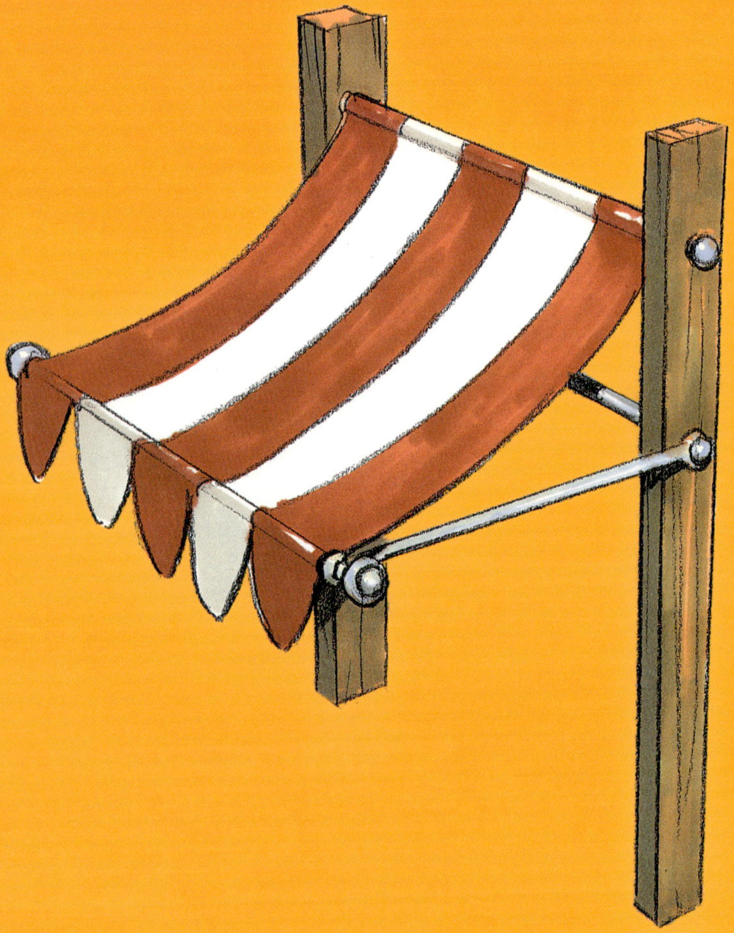

We put on
the roof.

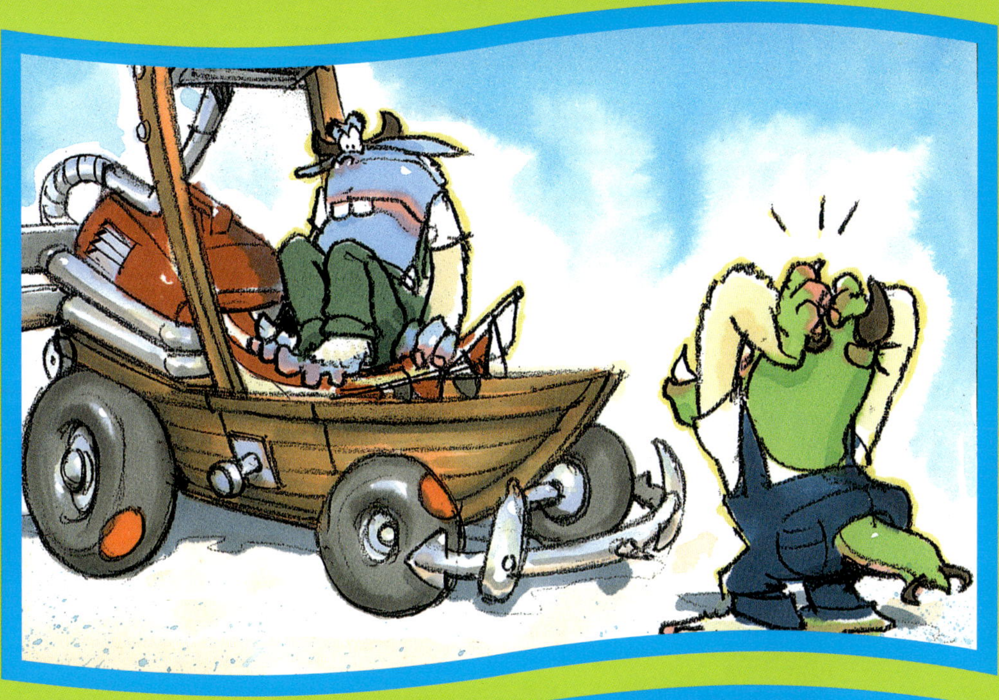

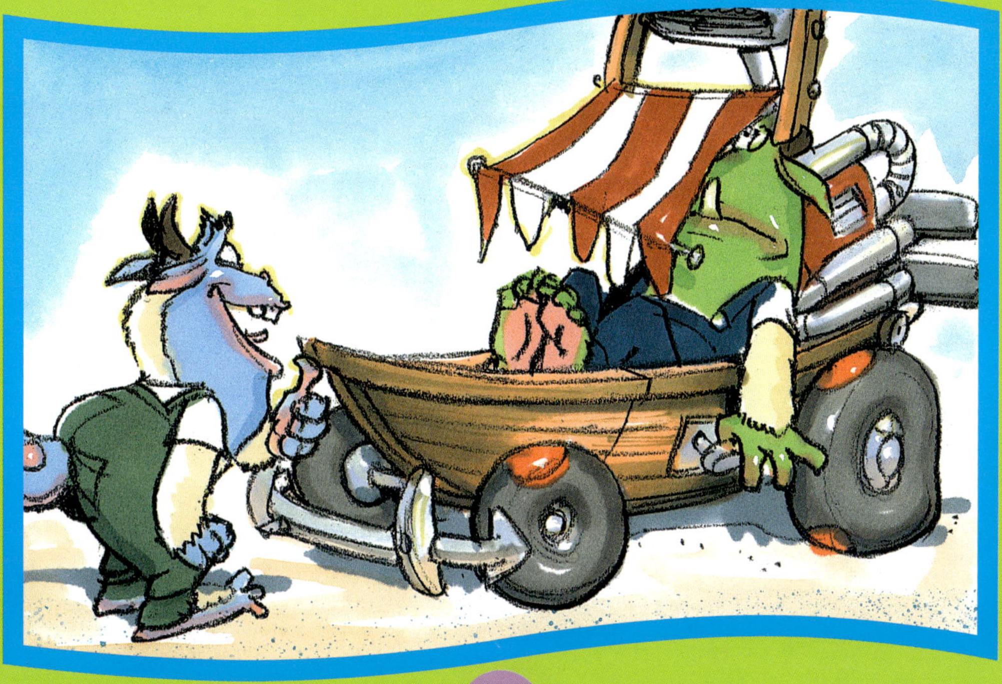

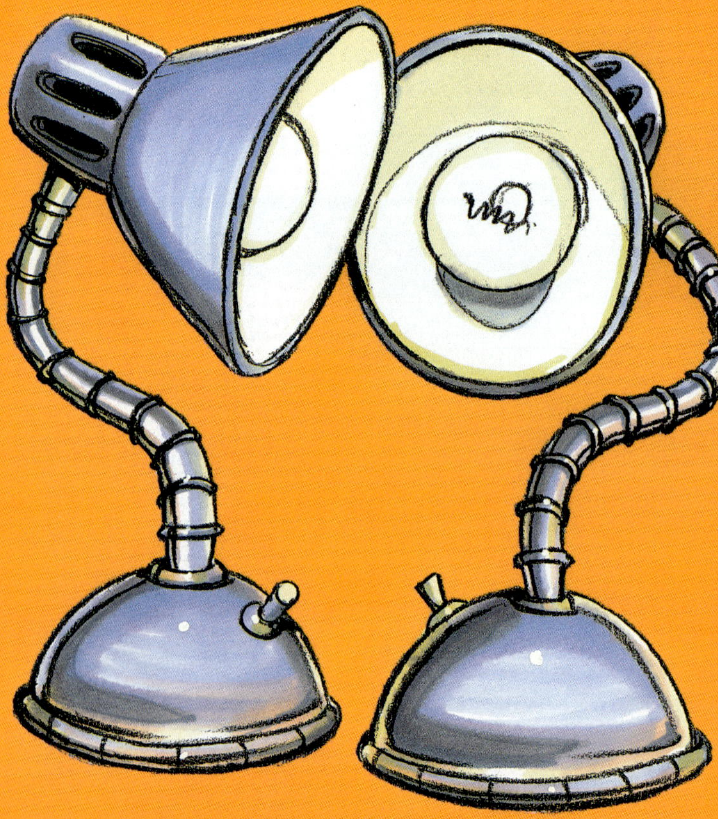

We put on
the lights.

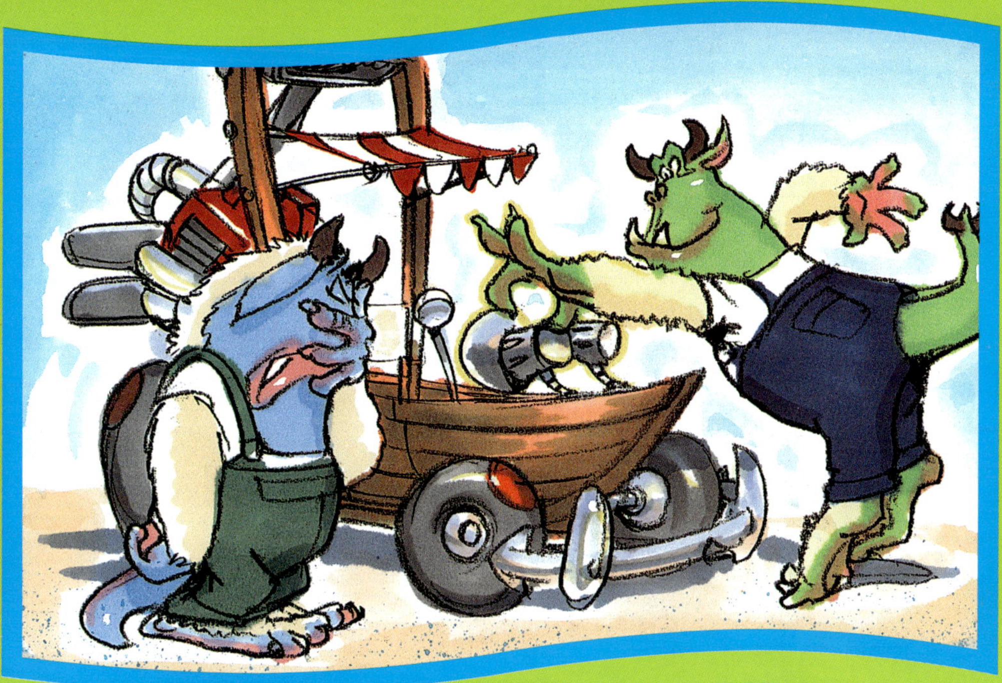

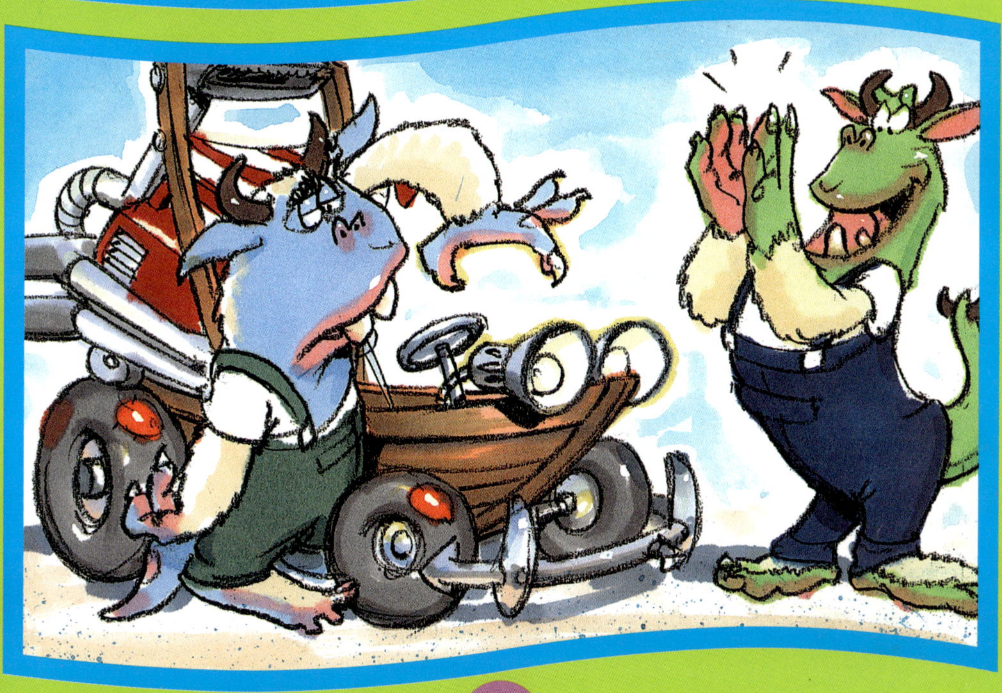

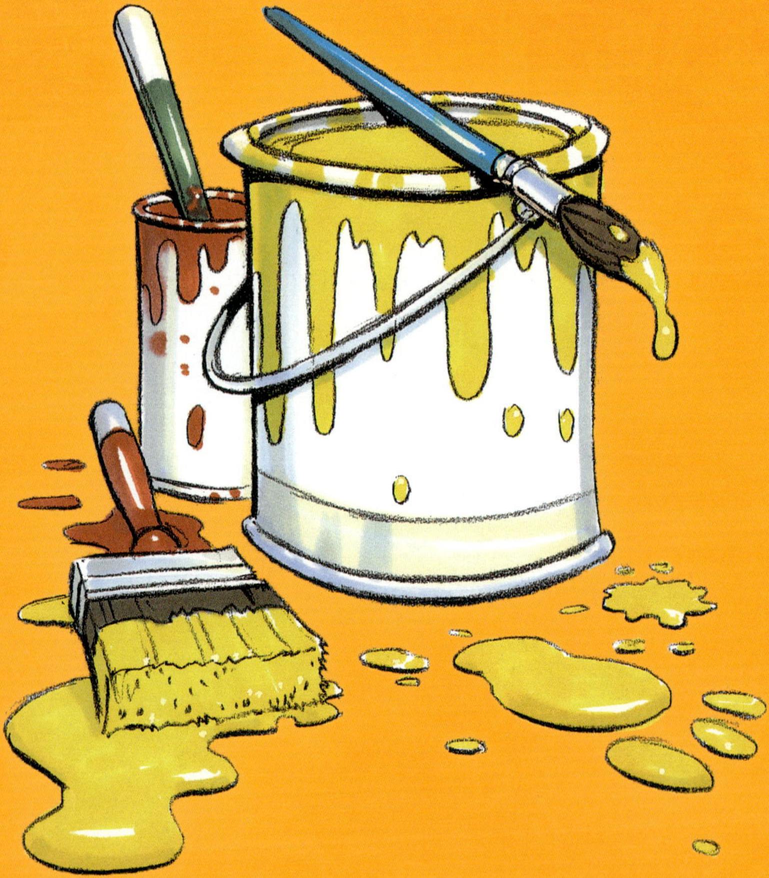

We put on
the paint.

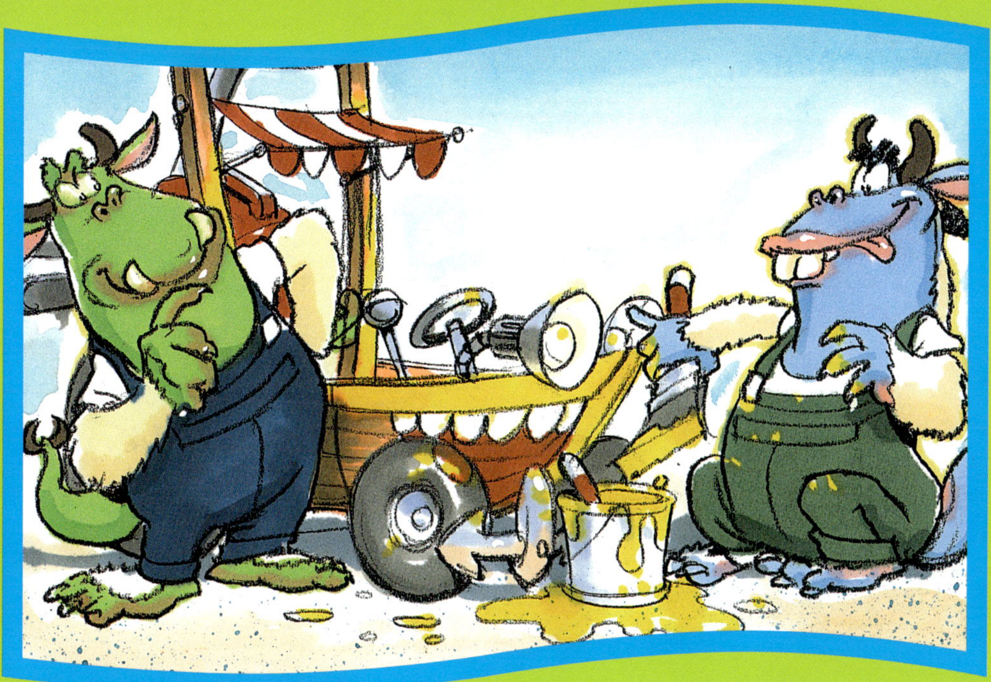

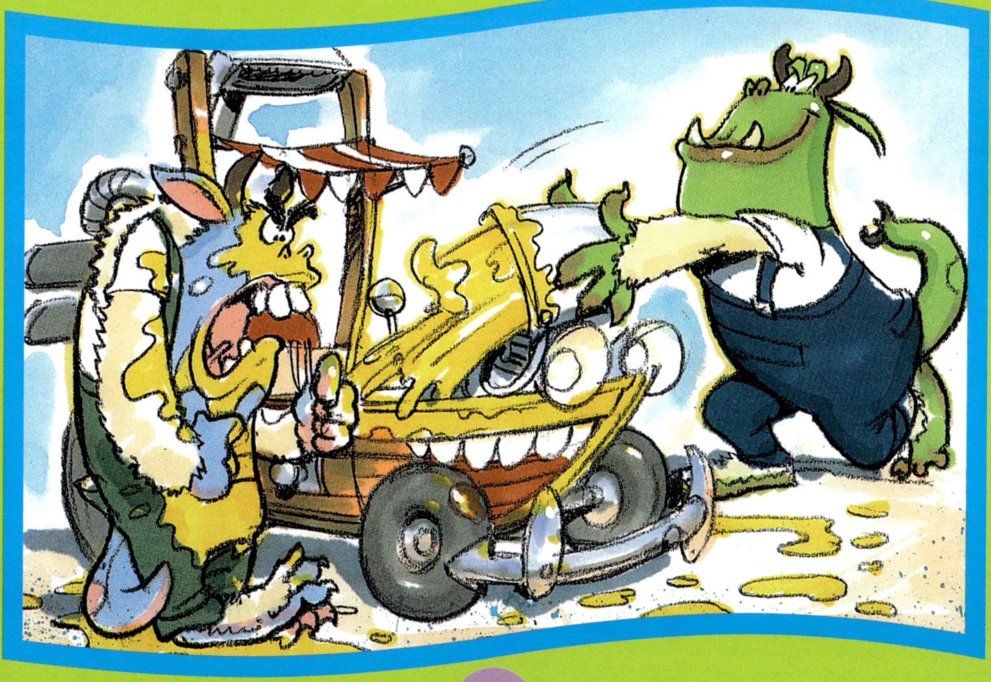

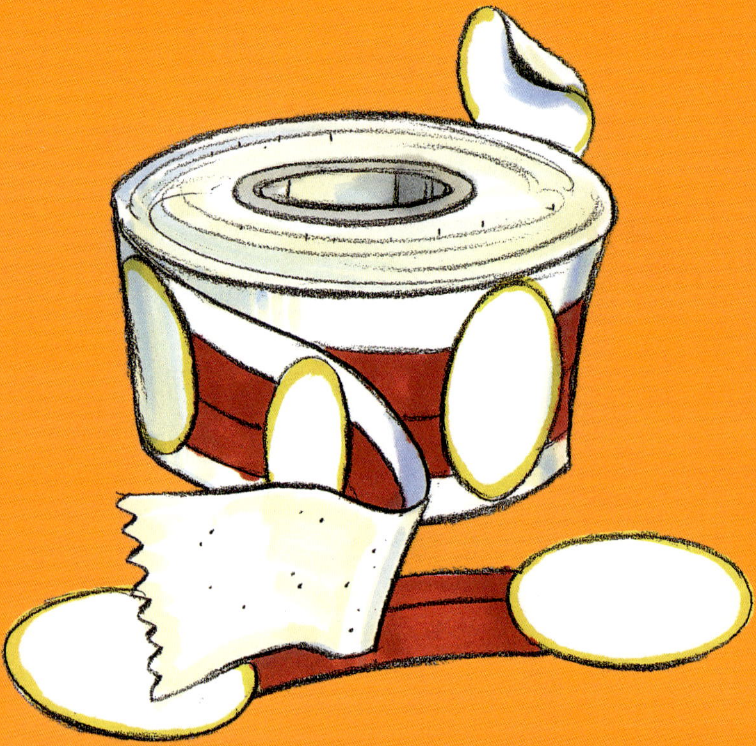

We put on
the spots.

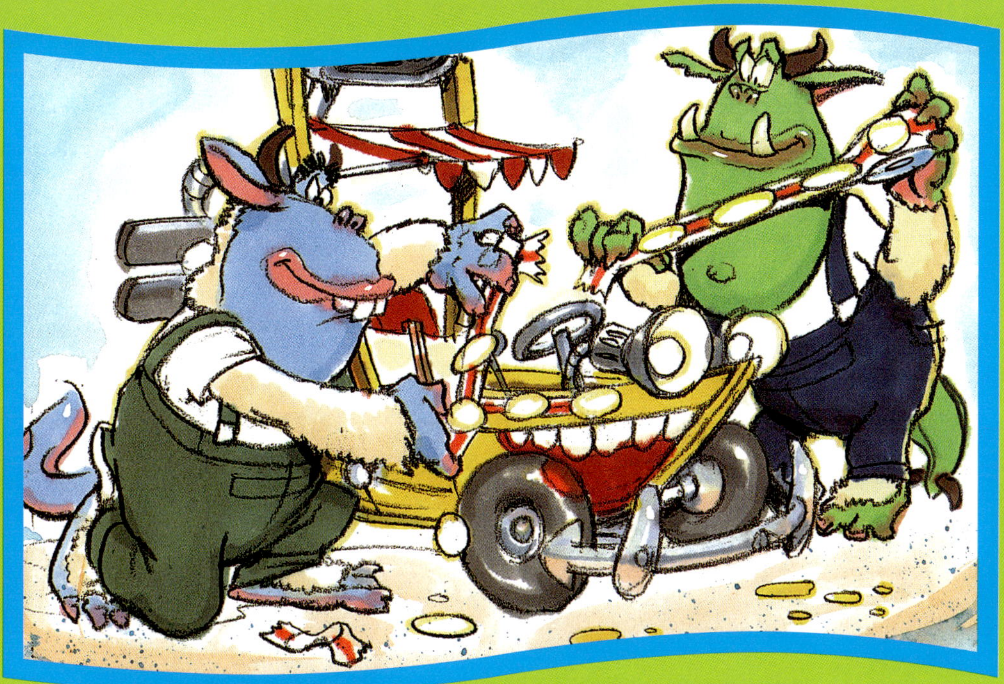

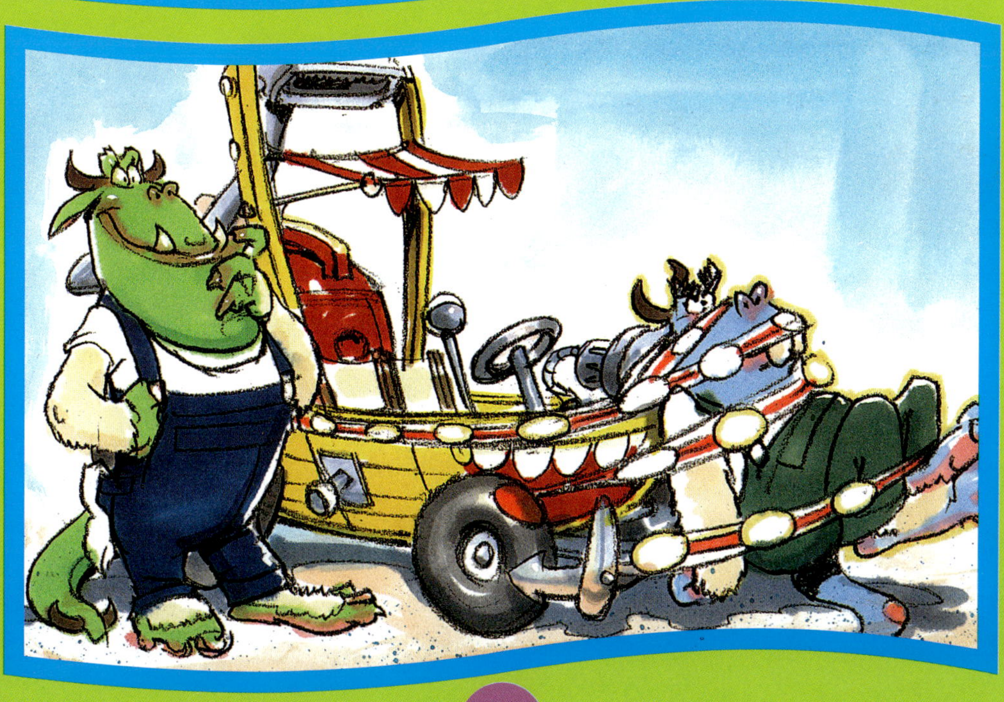

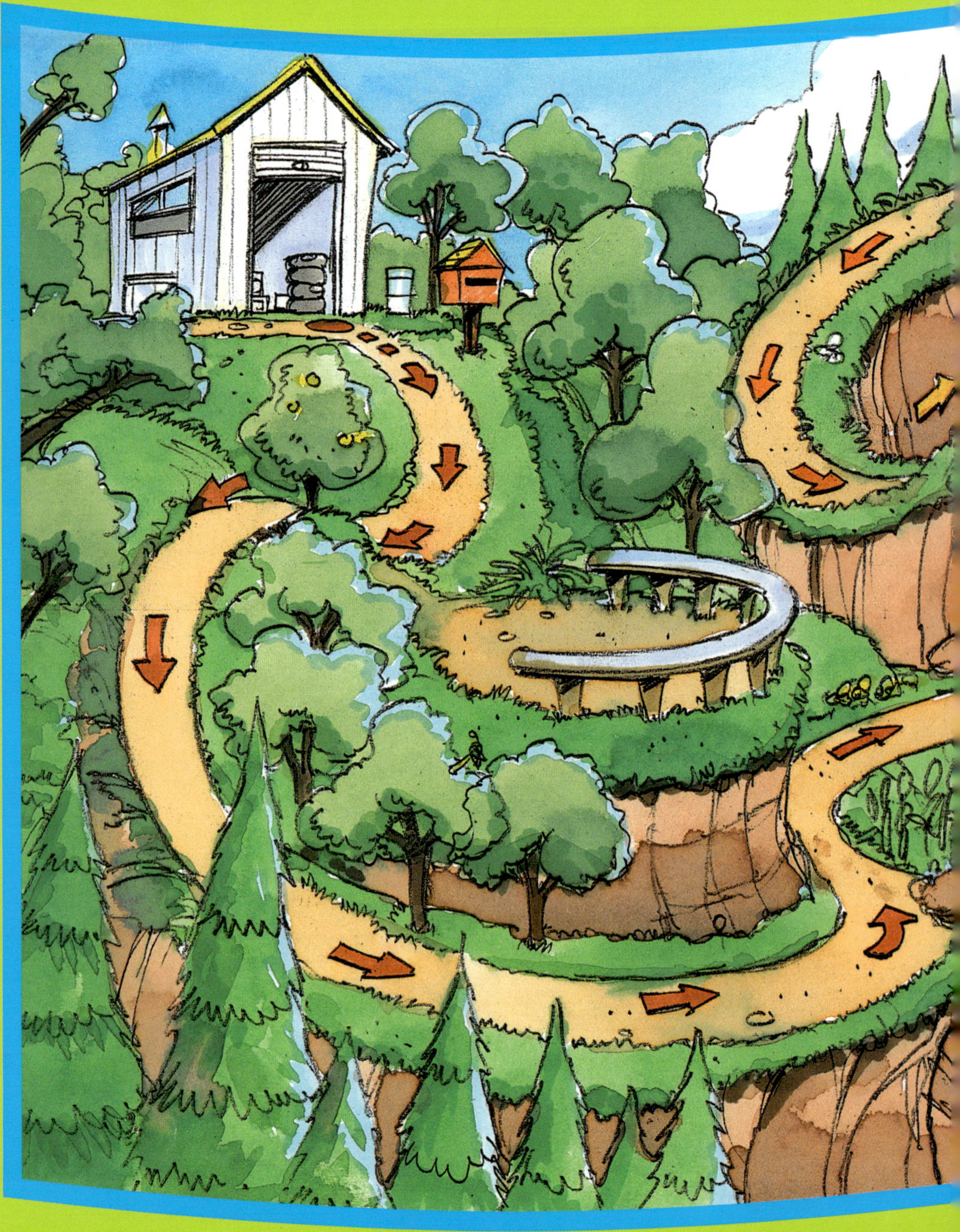

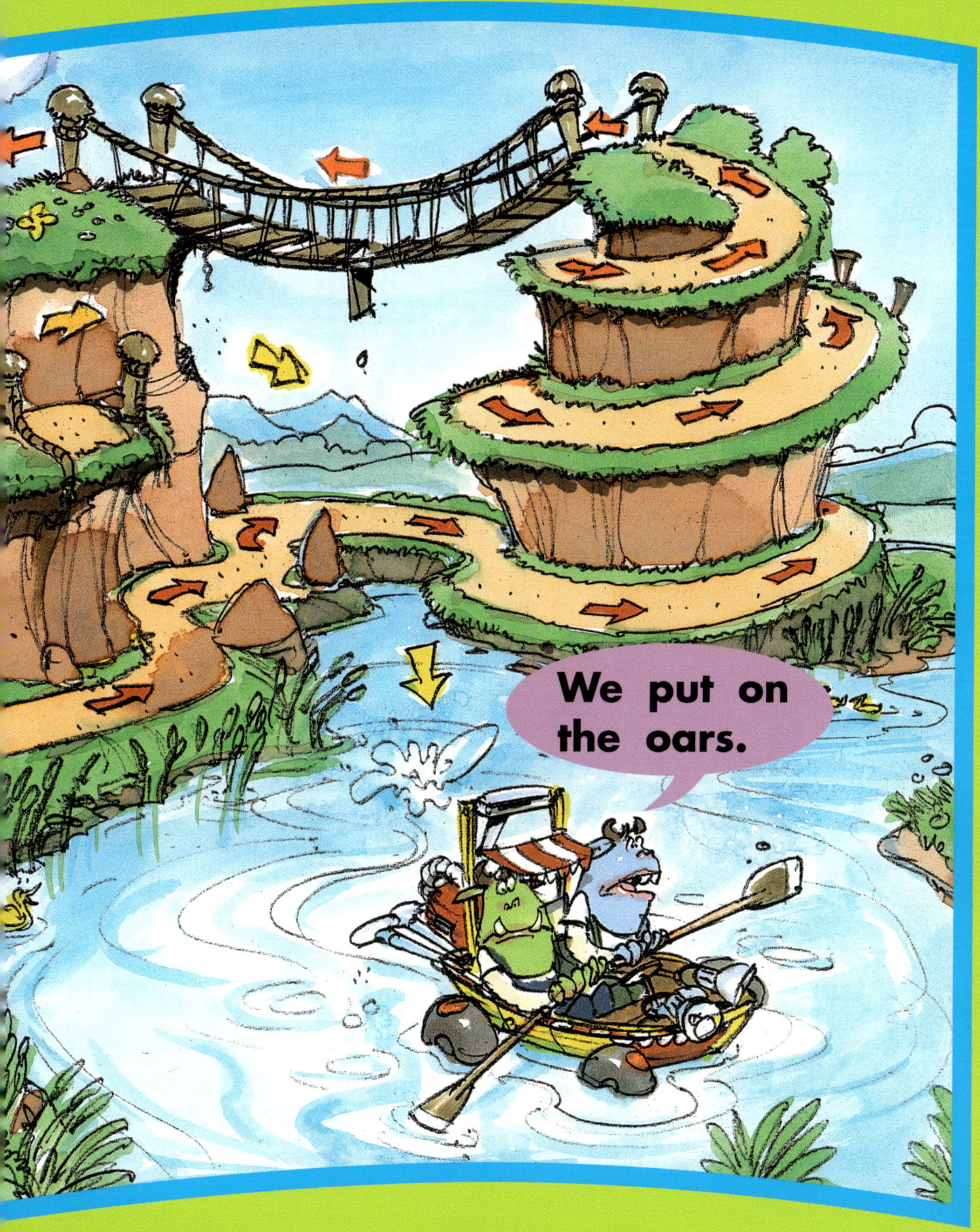
We put on the oars.

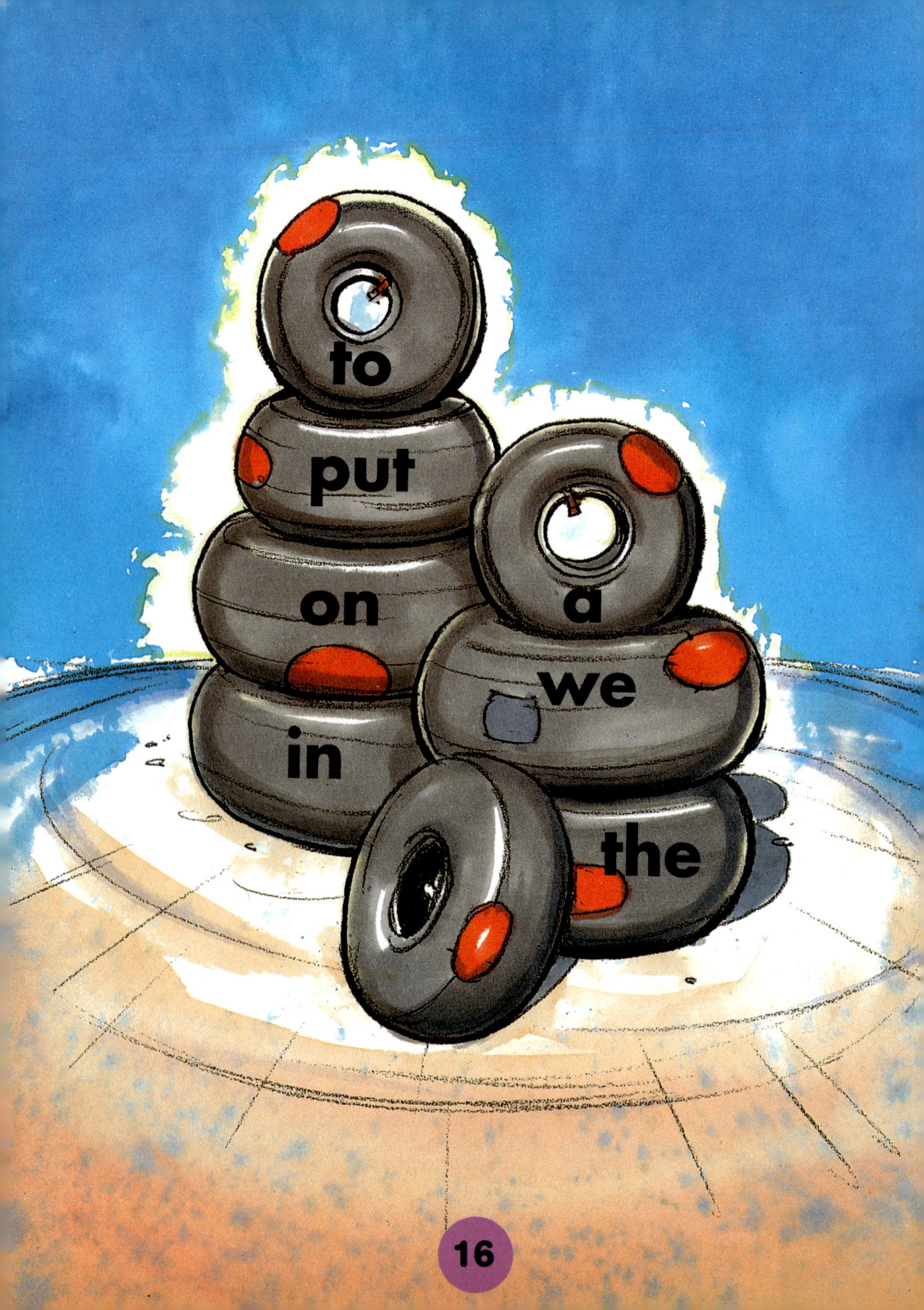
to
put
on
a
we
in
the